Salisbury

A Third Selection

IN OLD PHOTOGRAPHS

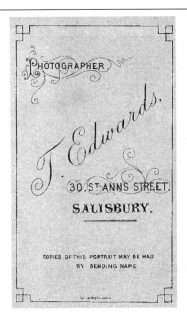

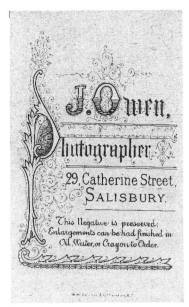

Examples of Victorian carte-de-visite photograph mounts used by four prominent Salisbury photographers.

Salisbury

A Third Selection

IN OLD PHOTOGRAPHS

Collected by PETER DANIELS

ALAN SUTTON

Alan Sutton Publishing Limited
Phoenix Mill · Far Thrupp · Stroud
Gloucestershire

First Published 1992

Copyright © Peter Daniels, 1992

British Library Cataloguing in Publication Data
A catalogue record for this book is available from
the British Library

Typeset in 9/10 Sabon.
Typesetting and origination by
Alan Sutton Publishing Limited.
Printed in Great Britain by
WBC Print Ltd, Bridgend.

Contents

Peter Daniels, 'The Old Picture Detective', in the driving seat of an 1892 Shand Mason horse-drawn fire-engine. Purchased from the chairman of East Knoyle Parish Council in 1947, this manual fire-pump is now safely preserved by Robert Burton of Salisbury. Brass fire-helmets are also rare collectors items today and this particular example is one of only half a dozen or so known to have survived locally. For many years it was part of a well known Salisbury volunteer fireman's kit. (Photograph courtesy of Russell Emm)

Introduction

This third volume of *Salisbury in Old Photographs* deals with the people, places, businesses, transport and other local interest items of our favoured city. The desire for knowledge of our local history, which has been growing over the past twenty years or so, is being encouraged, excited even, by the endeavour, research, detection and productions of Peter Daniels. What makes for special interest, particularly to those of mature years, are the memories engendered by his work. He is aware of so much; he should be – he has lived some of the history himself. He was at school and started his working life in this fair city. I hope his endeavours reap the reward they deserve.

Among the reactions to the previous books, as well as this, is one of nostalgia; this is excited in particular by the pictures of 'what once was' or of 'who used to be'. There is an element of regret, perhaps, for those who have not really forgotten, but there are surprises for readers who have recently settled here. Pictorial evidence survives of that which we have lost or have waved goodbye to: establishments and services such as our own police force and fire brigade as well as our water, electricity and gas supplies. There are more than a score of these 'No longer ours'.

The same is true of business houses run by private individuals or by families who were themselves citizens or, in many cases, City Fathers. Even our administration has changed during the period displayed. Is this progress?

While expressing regret for things past, though, bear in mind the improvements that have been made, such as the removal of the slum areas or the hard work and excellent results of such as Courts Ltd, by whose efforts decrepit cottages have become habitable and comfortable homes. The improvements are many.

Section Seven contains much on Fisherton Street, where the changes have been many. At one time this was the main thoroughfore, more so than High Street. The pressure of traffic was greater than in any other district, much of it, if not all, horsed transport in the earliest photographs. This was the result of there being two railway stations, the GWR and LSWR, at the west end of the street. There was a constant flow, towards and away from the town, of goods, commercial and pedestrian traffic. The passenger trains were full for fares were low. Besides, there were few alternatives then. The majority of these travellers by trains came to shop in our city, or to do business. The street could be filled with people, not only on the pavements but in the roadway.

Few of the businesses that were here in the times depicted still remain. Godwin's Footwear and Leather Merchants, and Futchers the Photographers can still be found today, but of the Magnet Stores the name alone survives. The photographs in this book, and in the earlier volumes, remind us of 'what was' and help us appreciate the advertisement painted on the upper wall of Mr Futcher's shop, now sadly erased: 'Secure the Shadow ere the Substance Fade.' Congratulations to Peter. He certainly is securing the shadows, much to our delight, and long may he continue.

Bill Garrett, Alderbury
September 1992

Scout Motor Company

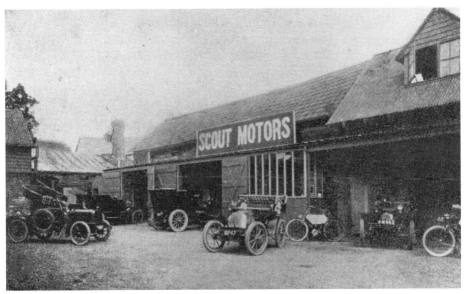

The Excelsior Works, Friary Lane, opened in 1901 by Albert and William Burden. Initially set up as a car repair workshop, agricultural and marine engines were being manufactured here after only a few weeks. In December 1903 the first Scout motorcycle was completed and delivered to Sidney Silverthorne, watchmaker, of 50 Catherine Street. It was allocated registration mark AM 65.

Albert Thomas Burden, joint founder of the Scout Motor Company. In around 1880 William Burden left Quarley, Hampshire and moved to Sandown Terrace, Salisbury to further develop his watchmaking trade. By 1896 the business had passed to his sons Albert Thomas and William Jun., and the company name was changed to Burden Brothers Ltd. A showroom was opened at 101 Fisherton Street and a manufactory taken on in the Wilton Road known as The Steam Clock Factory. By 1901, however, both sites had been vacated and the brothers inaugurated their motor repair workshop at 1 Friary Lane.

The First Scout car, with Joseph 'Percy' Dean at the wheel. Sales director of the firm from 1903 until around 1908, Mr Dean can be seen here, with Frank Farr, outside the carriage and motor body works at 55 Brown Street. The picture was taken in August 1905.

The Tourist Trophy car, at Douglas, Isle of Man, in 1905. Pictured above with AM 702 is Percy Dean and one of his firm's chief mechanics (Billy Lucas or Arthur Silk?). Only the second car to have been completed, this 14 hp side-entry model was turned out in double-quick time to replace the original TT car which is illustrated on the previous page. The first car was damaged beyond any immediate repair when it crashed near Wallop while being driven at moderate speed to Douglas, via Liverpool, very early one September morning. Unfortunately, despite its admirable performance, the replacement car ran out of petrol and came to a halt just short of the finishing line. Of the forty-two cars which started the race, only eighteen managed to complete the 208 mile circuit on the allocated 9¹/₂ gallons of fuel.

Number Ten, a standard four-cylinder side-entry model for Richard Charles Baker of Hurdcott House, Wiltshire. On 24 July 1906 this green-painted car was given registration mark AM 892, the tenth chassis to be manufactured at the Friary Lane works. Another of Mr Baker's fine cars can be seen on page 153 of *Around Wilton in Old Photographs* by the same author.

A car for special occasions. This smart 20 hp Brougham was assembled in 1907 for Frederick Peacock Papps. It was one of several Scout vehicles which he 'let out on hire'. The chocolate-coloured body was made at Farr's coach works in Brown Street.

The main machine shop at the new motor works, 1907. A set of plans submitted to Wilton Rural District Council on 15 July 1906 was approved without too much delay, and soon afterwards construction work began on this large, purpose-built factory in Churchfields Road, Bemerton.

Better than riding a bike. Louis Conio is in the driving seat of AM 1691, a 24 hp side-entry model purchased by John Nash & Sons, cycle and motor engineers of 82–4 Castle Street, in June 1910. Upholstered in green leather, the car was painted white with fine green lines picking out the bonnet, doors, wings and wheels.

A businessman's car. In 1912 William Main ordered this shining new landaulette, AM 2564, a 25 hp car with dark blue paintwork and matching blue leather upholstery. Residing at Grosvenor House, Churchfields Road, Mr Main traded as a corn merchant, with a store at 108 Fisherton Street and a shop at 22 Minster Street.

The First World War: a time of good and bad fortune. In 1915 much of the works' machinery was commandeered and sent to France for on-the-spot maintenance of military vehicles. In the same year J. Percy Dean and his successor, C.H. Radcliffe, lost their lives in tragic circumstances. The firm prospered, however, through its lucrative government contracts. Rosa Bailey is pictured above machining parts for magnetic mines.

The grey lady. A glimpse at this stylish Medusa Grey Scout Torpedo will certainly not turn you to stone; it is a thing of beauty. One can easily imagine the elegance of this fine car with its blue leather upholstery, brass radiator surround and brass lamps. In May 1913 this 15.9 hp car was delivered to Mr Amrose Tucker of Hillcote, 22 Manor Road, Salisbury.

The first two-ton Scout delivery van was sold to Hardy & Son of Catherine Street. The catalogue price for a canvas-tilt van, painted and lettered as illustrated, was just £585. The vehicle was allocated registration mark AM 1652 on 10 October 1910.

A carrier's enterprise. For very many years Victor White travelled the roads between Hurstbourne Tarrant, Newbury and Andover carrying on the trade of a country carrier. In 1911 he laid up his faithful old horse in favour of motor traction, something of a novelty in the country carrying business at the time. A lack of funds prevented him from buying a completely new van, so he simply ordered this chassis from Scout Motors, to which was fitted his old horse-drawn cart (minus its wheels and axles). Listed in the Hampshire hackney-carriage register, AA 2394 is pictured here at Newbury.

Opposite: Tea and coffee tastefully transported. This pretty little 10 hp van was the first commercial vehicle to be turned out of the Scout Motor Works at Bemerton. It was delivered to Robert Stokes' New Canal warehouse in June 1908. The dark blue paintwork contrasted very tastefully with the silver lettering. It was not a machine built for speed: it featured a two-cylinder engine and solid rubber tyres at the rear.

On the Brighton run. This 37 hp Scout motor bus was one of five similar machines ordered by Wilts and Dorset Motor Services in 1915. After running in the Salisbury area for a short time, IB 805 was transfered to Southdown Motor Services.

An important government contract? Wort and Way was a well-known Salisbury firm employed on government work. During the First World War they ran a large fleet of steam wagons and petrol lorries, including a few Scouts. This particular one worked at the weekend too.

Commercial life in Cromer. Scout Motors secured an order for this attractive one-ton van despite some very keen competition. A good deal of interest was taken in the machine throughout its early working life with Rusts of Norfolk; in 1913 it appeared several times in *Commercial Motor* magazine.

A late charabanc. The production of domestic and industrial Scout vehicles was resumed in 1919, albeit at a greatly reduced level. One of only a few vehicles to be turned out in 1920, this twenty-nine-seater Torpedo Charabanc joined the Annetts and Porter fleet at Tidworth. It displayed Hampshire registration mark HO 8263.

Sir Cecil Chubb's coupé, HR 3561. Supplied in August 1920, this 15.9 hp, two-seat, royal blue, fixed coupé was Sir Cecil's fourth and last Scout car. The Scout Motor Company was in serious financial trouble by this date, and in June 1921 it was voluntarily wound up.

Scout sentimentality. Originally supplied to a Hampshire motor dealer, this 15.9 hp side-entry car is one of only three Scout machines known to have survived. After taking part in a motor rally in 1953 it was stored in a garage in Yeovil where it lay neglected and forgotten for thirty-one years. It was re-discovered by the author in 1984 and while attempts were made to secure it for all the people of Salisbury it was snapped up by a local businessman.

SECTION TWO

Fire Brigades

The Salisbury Municipal Fire Brigade was established in 1853. It was the best equipped and most professionally trained fire-fighting force in the city at the time. The brigade was composed of a superintendent, a deputy superintendent and eighteen firemen. William Pearce was the first superintendent. The list of appliances kept at the engine house in Catherine Street included a horse-drawn 7 inch manual pump, 700 feet of leather hose, a selection of ladders and numerous other pieces of equipment. Reproduced above is the oldest known photograph depicting the entire Salisbury brigade; it was taken in front of the Red Lion Hotel in Milford Street.

Water in the Canal. Between the years 1848 and 1859 the ancient street watercourses were covered over and a new pumping station was constructed on Bishopdown Hill. This new high pressure water system not only benefited the inhabitants of Salisbury, but also greatly improved the efficiency of the Municipal Fire Brigade. This early photograph shows quite clearly how the piped water was used to keep the dust down in the Pig Market area of New Canal. For many years the building shown in the background was known as the Victoria Temperance Hotel.

The Salisbury Volunteer Fire Brigade (SVFB) was inaugurated at the Red Lion Hotel on 17 July 1884. The initial company of twenty-four men was commanded by Captain Frederick Style (top left). He was probably better known, however, for his association with the large emporium in Blue Boar Row known as Style and Gerrish. Top right: Edward Wilkes Gawthorne, first lieutenant of SVFB and former proprietor of the Red Lion Hotel. Right: fireman Charles Lefevre, in his fire kit, who served with the brigade until 1903.

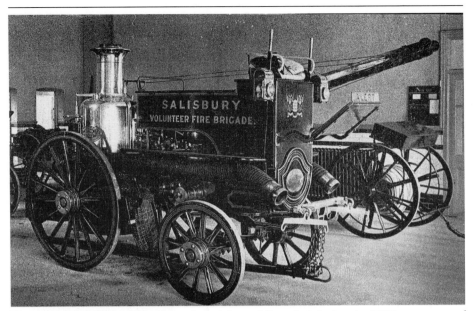

The steam fire-engine *Alert*, purchased by public subscription in 1891 at a cost of £585 11s. Manufactured by Merryweather and Sons of Greenwich, this double-cylinder pump could deliver 360 gallons per minute. The appliance carried the SVFB motto 'Semper Paratus' (Always Prepared).

The old 7 inch manual engine, adopted by the SVFB when the Municipal Brigade was disbanded in 1889. On this occasion the appliance was manned by Coachman Feltham, Engineer Fawcett, and Firemen Dawes and Newton.

The Hose Cart, 1893. This appliance carried a hand pump, several lengths of canvas hose, standpipes, branches, four scaling ladders and numerous other tools. In a local emergency this was generally the first apparatus to leave the station. Firemen J. Bothwell and A.E. Rawlings are at the head of the cart, and at the back is E.W. Gawthorne who was promoted to captain in 1886.

Fireman Bingham and the Hose-reel Cart, in front of the Council Chamber (now the Guildhall) in 1893. The eight lengths of hose carried on this appliance can be seen coiled around the axle. The requisite standpipes, branches and tools were stored in the container above. Second Officer E.C. Hardy stands on the right.

The charred remains of Mr Vibert's grocery shop, 1901. On 24 May an overwhelming con-flagration destroyed Ware Brothers' Leather Works at the back of 4 Endless Street, in Three Swans Chequer. The blaze spread rapidly and sparks were blown all around the neighbouring streets, where numerous secondary outbreaks took hold. The most serious of these was at B. Vibert's grocery and wine & spirit shop at 22 Oatmeal Row. The building was totally destroyed, allowing a rare view of Minster Street directly from the Market Place.

The new fire station in Salt Lane, 1907. Erected on the site of the original engine house, the building was commissioned by Salisbury Corporation, at a cost of £1,700. Having been enlarged and improved several times over the years, the building was finally vacated in 1964 when the Ashley Road Fire Station was opened.

The inauguration ceremony was performed on 1 May 1907. The Mayor, Mr Samuel Grove, and members of the Corporation are heading for the Market Place to join thousands of spectators who had gathered there to watch a water pumping demonstration based on the steam fire-engine.

A wheeled escape ladder at the English Clock Factory. Very little remained of Williamsons' clock manufactory in Southampton Road after it was engulfed in flames on 27 May 1909. More recently this was the site of Newman's Garage where the author served as an apprentice in the 1960s.

The Salt Lane appliance room, 1910. The Steam Fire-engine *Alert* stands between a 29 foot telescopic Horsed Fire-escape (left) and Hose and Ladder Cart No. 2. The brigade's 50 foot wheeled fire-escapes were parked outside the Infirmary and the Council Chamber because they were too large to be housed in the fire station itself.

King George V's coronation celebrations, 1911. Three appliances were displayed in front of the Council Chamber: the telescopic Horsed Fire-escape on the left, the Steam Fire-engine in the centre and the 6 inch Manual Engine to the right.

Salisbury's first motor fire-engine, 1913. Based on a 50 hp Commercar chassis, the appliance was equipped by Henry Simonis & Company of London. A rear-mounted 360 gallon-per-minute pump and a 30 gallon water tank were installed. The vehicle also carried 150 feet of hose and a 50 foot wheeled escape ladder. It was named *Fawcett* as a memorial to former brigade captain Sydney Fawcett, who died in 1904.

The *Fawcett*'s first public performance, 29 January 1913. The machine was set to work in the Market Place where thousands of local people had turned out to enjoy the watery spectacle. Fireman Walter Letheren couples up lengths of hose in the foreground.

Motor Tender No. 2. Based on a second-hand 1906 Humber motor hearse chassis, AM 3763 was acquired by SVFB in 1914. It carried a 29 foot Bailey wheeled fire-escape, several lengths of delivery hose and a selection of tools.

Salisbury Steam Laundry destroyed, 12 June 1922. The full extent of the tragedy can be seen clearly: charred timbers and pieces of twisted metal lie in all directions. Damage to the factory and loss of customers' goods was estimated to be around £40,000. Coincidentally, there had been a fire at the laundry exactly thirty years earlier, in June 1892.

Station keeper Bill Miggins with the *Frank Baker*. This attractive fire-fighting combination was manufactured by the Tilling Stevens Company of Maidstone, Kent in 1924 and it carried their chassis number 5,000. Taken on as appliance No. 3, this 28 hp motor tender and Bantam trailer pump benefited from all the latest devices and improvements (metal disc wheels, pneumatic tyres, electric lighting). It was allocated Wiltshire registration mark MR 205. A brass plaque fitted below the windscreen was engraved with the name Frank Baker, mayor of Salisbury 1905/6. This was a tribute to a benevolent man who did so much for the city he loved. His most noted charitable success was the first Salisbury Hospital Carnival, which raised a large sum of money in June 1906.

The *Fawcett* in festive mood. The seven-hundreth anniversary of the New Sarum Charter was celebrated in June 1927. The *Fawcett* motor tender follows the Band of the 4th Battalion the Wiltshire Regiment as the carnival procession moves sedately along Crane Street.

A snapshot of *The Chief*, 1930s. Despite a thorough search by the Old Picture Detective a good clear photograph of MW 6125 could not be found. The appliance was made in 1930 by the well-known fire-engine manufacturer, Dennis Brothers of Guildford. SVFB named it *The Chief*.

The Chairman at the Council Chamber, before the Second World War. WV 3933 was a quality fire appliance manufactured by Dennis Brothers in 1933. It featured a 350/450 gallon-per-minute pump and a 50 foot wheeled fire-escape. Charlie Acton and Reg Robbins are the two firemen standing on the machine, and among their colleagues are George Hardy, George Wallis and Jack Wort.

SVFB Golden Jubilee celebrations, 29 July 1934. Past and present volunteers marched to the Cathedral for a service of thanksgiving. After a midday luncheon an assortment of old and new fire-engines was paraded around the city streets.

King George V's Silver Jubilee celebrations, Monday 6 May 1935. The Salisbury fire-engine of 1770 arrived safely back at Victoria Park after taking part in the carnival procession. With the relic are Frank Harfitt, William Humby, Nelson Morris and Alfred Morris.

The day after the fire. The Salisbury Co-operative Society furnishing store on the corner of Milford Street and Queen Street was destroyed by fire on Monday 13 September 1937. The well-trained Salisbury volunteers successfully contained the outbreak and prevented it from spreading to neighbouring properties.

A fireman's wedding. Salisbury firemen form a guard of honour at St Paul's church for their newlywed colleague Albert Noyce and his bride Dorothy. The happy couple were married just three days before war was declared on 3 September 1939. In the evening a reception was held at the Morrison Hall in Milford Street, which was just a few doors away from Mr Noyce's tobacconist shop.

Opposite: Pump drill on Fisherton Bridge, involving the personnel of Devizes Road AFS Station. On the far side of the bridge the Maundrel Hall was being used as a Servicemen's Institute. At the time of writing an Argos showroom occupies the site.

Wartime firefighters. The No. 1 Auxiliary Fire Station was set up at the former Walls ice cream depot in Devizes Road, on the site of the old jail ground (last used 1859), near the junction with Gas Lane. Back row (left to right): S. Haines, W.P. Winchcombe, E. Goulding, E. Flemington, G. Sweetlove, T. Price, C. Taylor, W. Enticott. Middle row: E.H. Lloyd, J.J. Vickers, C.E. Kyte, H.N. Topham, G. Maple, E.A. Canning, C.V. Sherlock, F. Case, H. Welch, R. Dawkins, W. Walton, E.G. Davidge, G. Millhench. Front row: W. Abel, N.H. Austin, B. Bevan, C.N. Higgins (section-officer), H. Roles (sub-officer), H. Wilkins, D. Hammond.

Fire Force 39 in Wyndham Road. Station X was set up soon after the SVFB became part of the National Fire Service on 18 August 1941. Trailer pumps like the ones here were generally pulled by government issued Austin K4 and Fordson V8 towing units, or indeed any available vehicle. Caffyn's car showrooms are on this site today.

Auxiliary Fire Service pumps in Blue Boar Row, returning to station following a services demonstration in the Market Place.

Too good to lose. These two delightful Salisbury old timers stand on display at a fire-engine rally in August 1979. Both machines have been safely preserved. The appliance nearest the camera is a 1939 Leyland 100 foot turntable ladder which was originally supplied to Bristol Fire Brigade. After serving that city for a reletively short time, however, the vehicle was transferred to Salisbury. Its original Bristol registration mark, GHW 415, was retained. The second machine is a Dennis F12 pump-escape, HMR 765, supplied to Wiltshire Fire Brigade in 1951 and stationed at Salisbury. This impressive appliance was fitted with a Rolls Royce B80 model 8-cylinder petrol engine. A Dennis pump was mounted amidships (with coupling points on each side of the body) and it carried a wheeled fire-escape.

The first post-war fire-engine. Based on the Commer 21A chassis, with bodywork by James Whitson & Co. Ltd of Yiewsley, West Drayton, the water tender was one of three similar appliances supplied to Wiltshire Fire Brigade in 1950: GMW 526 served at Salisbury, GMW 953 was stationed at Ludgershall and GWV 377 was allocated to Swindon. The Salisbury appliance, which remained in service until 1972, has survived and is presently being cared for by an enthusiast.

SECTION THREE

Scenes Around the Town

A panoramic view from the spire of Salisbury Cathedral, 1903. In the middleground stand St Thomas's church, the Electric Light Works and St Thomas's Elementary School, which was erected in 1858. The Wilts and Dorset Bank (now Lloyds) can be seen to the right. Pictured to the left is the Congregational church, Maundrel Hall and Williams Brothers' malt houses, with Old Sarum on the skyline beyond.

Salisbury Cathedral from the west, 1897. Some essential repair work was being carried out on the tower and spire, and an appeal was launched to finance the project. Typical of many local fund-raising events, a large and influential public meeting was held on 28 January 1896 at the County Hall in Endless Street. Presided over by the mayor, Arthur Russell Malden, £100 was collected and many promises given. The picture was taken by Clement Osmond (a monumental mason).

Salisbury Cathedral from Palace Park, 1935. How often these days would you see a cow being milked within the walls of the Cathedral close? Bishop Lovett vacated the Bishop's Palace in 1946 and in the following year the building and grounds were taken over by the Cathedral School.

Opposite: A stroll along West Walk, 1910. Ven. Archdeacon Buchanan's residence, the North Canonry, can be seen in the distance. Out of view to the right is Arundells, the present home of former prime minister Sir Edward Heath, which was occupied at the time by Lady Ellen Gordon.

An Edwardian view of North Walk. The motor car parked outside Nos 20 and 21 appears to be AM 1232, a green coloured 12 hp tonneau which Scout Motors supplied to Doctor Luckham of 47 Winchester Street in July 1908. Perhaps the doctor was making a house call on Revd Canon Sir James Erasmus Bt or Revd Precentor Harry William Carpenter.

St Ann's Gate, 1906. 'Take Notice; "All Wagons, Carts and Timber Carriages, Sheep, Pigs and Cattle are prohibited from passing through, and all Horses from being exercised within the Close of Sarum." By order of the Dean and Chapter.' This young lad may have been delivering papers such as the *Salisbury and Winchester Journal* or *Salisbury Times* for newsagent George Gilbert.

The oldest known view of St Ann Street, probably taken in the 1870s. Two of Lovibond's horse-drawn brewery wagons can be seen outside Charles Perkins' ale house. Next-door, at No. 38, one can just decipher the following words: W. Adey, Builder. The ancient houses on the left have gone.

St John Street during the First World War. Folliott's horse-drawn dray can be seen delivering ale to the Kings Arms Inn. Many changes have taken place here: Clement Osmond's masonry workshop is now Gilberts Newsagents, and George Gilbert's original shop now forms part of the Kings Arms Hotel.

Catherine Street, 1906. A wardrobe dealer named Miss Wilson ran the shop on the extreme left of the picture and Henry Smith managed the boot warehouse next-door. His immediate neighbour was Francis Newton, who ran a sub-post office in addition to dispensing 'cures'. On the opposite corner of Antelope Square, where the Antique and Flea Market is today, Dunfords were in business as drapers, dressmakers, milliners, glovers and hosiers. On the other side of the street one could find Harry Earle's confectionery shop as well as Fowler and Bailey (linen), Frank Simmonds (cabinet-maker), E.W. Judd (butcher) and The City Tailoring Company, where Arthur Oliver was the manager.

The Priory, Brown Street, 1904. For many years this was the residence of George Main and family. Mrs Main stands at the gate with her daughter Violet, who later married Dr Gilbert Kempe of 17 Endless Street. Their coachman was Frederick Franklin, who lived at 7 St Ann Street.

Milford Street, 1920s. The Oddfellows Arms Inn (licensee, Frank Francis) and the Red Lion Hotel (proprietor, Charles Thomas) can be seen to the left. Nearest the camera on the right is the Round of Beef (demolished before 1930). The Ford van is parked outside Jesse Denham's Bakery, which is now part of Chas H. Baker & Son's premises.

The Canal, early this century. The Head Post Office is on the left, vacated in March 1907 when the new post office building was opened in Castle Street. In the last century Pritchard & Clark, on the right, was a respectable supplier of ladies' corsets. The store had closed by 1907 and Lord & Farmer occupy the premises today.

The Pig Market, New Canal, 1886. Left of centre is Young and Brinsmead's piano and harmonium repair shop (their showrooms were at 2/3 Queen Street). A taxi rank can be found here today, and on Tuesday and Saturday each week this is where the country buses congregate. Behind the trees stood the Roe Buck Inn, where Dorchester ales and stouts were served. Flying the flag on the right is the Victoria Temperance Hotel.

A place for soldiers during the First World War. Formerly occupied by solicitors Harding and Hall, 39 The Canal was converted into a free guest house for visiting soldiers. From the early 1930s until around 1968 the Bay Tree Tea Rooms were here, established by Mrs Frances Weedon. The site is now the Salisbury Methodist Church Charity Shop.

The Crown Hotel, 1953. Established in 1625 and situated at 46/8 High Street, the hotel's resident proprietor from 1921 until 1945 was Edwin Whitby. At the time of this photograph Mrs Whitby was the manageress. The business survived until around 1969.

High Street, 1880. The White Hart Hotel parcels van appears to be parked outside No. 15, the premises of Alfred Kemm, a carver, woodworker, maker of artistic furniture, and dealer in antique furniture and old china. Across the road at No. 40, Henry Neesham managed his religious tract depot.

Crane Street, 1910. Noyes and Green (established 1900) are immediately to the left, followed by Frederick Sutton's Bakery and Tea Room and the County Weights and Measures Office. On the other side of the street the Crown Hotel staff entrance can be seen, as well as the double doors of the hotel garage, over which was fixed an enamel sign advertising the business of W.R. Whereat, a cabinet-maker of 45 The Canal.

Crane Bridge and Church House, 1935. The bridge has been widened twice since 1898 and on each occasion a commemorative stone was built into the structure. The first is engraved with the following words: 'This side of the bridge was taken down and rebuilt 7 feet further south, in the year 1898. Howard Harris Mayor.' The second memorial exhibits the name H. Rackham, City Engineer: 'The bridge was widened a further 14 feet on its south side in the year 1970.'

A flood in Harcourt Bridge Road, 1915. The brougham can be seen outside the Nurses Home, now known as Harcourt House. The dwelling in the distance (8 Mill Road) was the residence of John Beresford (boot-maker). His neighbours were Albert Thomas Burden (Scout Motor Company) and James Sanger (tallow chandler, Harham Mill).

London & South Western Railway Station, 1925. The advertising posters reveal that special trains were scheduled for people wishing to visit the Royal Tournament at Olympia or the British Empire Exhibition at Wembley. An engraved stone on the station façade is dated 1881.

A birds-eye view of waiting cabs at the L&SWR Station, 1908. Among the assembled vehicles are horse-drawn buses from the County Hotel, Red Lion Hotel and Angel Hotel. The White Hart parcels van can also be seen. The station-master's house and the District Goods Office are gone.

The Milk Factory chimney. In the 1920s the plant was known as Fussells Condensed Milk Factory, but by 1927 the name had changed to the Nestlé & Anglo Swiss Condensed Milk Factory. The buildings were demolished in around 1987 and houses stand on the site today.

The Hydasoc Milk Factory from the air. Hydasoc was the trading name of the Hygienic Dairy Society Limited who opened their factory in Russell Street (now Russell Road) before 1908. Devizes Road can be seen across the top of the picture.

Devizes Road, 1914. On the right is Miss Mary Kelly's post office and general store. Still to be seen on the side of the building are a few partly obliterated words which probably read as follows: STO(p here for) CONF(ectionery) COOK(ed meats). By 1927 the post office had moved up the road to No. 220.

St Paul's Road, 1907. All the buildings on the north side, including Fisherton Anger School (built 1890), were demolished in around 1969/70 and replaced by the four-lane Churchill Way relief road. During the early years of the century this part of Salisbury was known as 'Railway Town' because of the large number of railway employees who lived in the area.

Victoria Park, 1902. Pleasantly situated at the junction of the Amesbury and Stratford Roads, the park was opened in 1887 as a memorial of Queen Victoria's Golden Jubilee. The grounds were laid out with gardens, a cycle track, a football ground and stand, a bowling green, a putting green and tennis courts. Unfortunately, the bandstand was taken down many years ago.

Castle Street, before 1880. The inferior optical quality of many early carte-de-visite photographs is demonstrated by this badly faded example. It is, nevertheless, still very interesting. Most of the buildings to the right survive, but those to the left have gone.

Castle Street in the nineteenth century. Selina Curtis kept the general store on the corner of Castle Street and Chipper Lane for over thirty years until Miss Fanny Curtis took over as proprietor around 1889. Shortly after closing her shop for the last time in 1900 the building was demolished and new regional offices were built on the site for the Wilts and Dorset Banking Company (opened 1901). At least two other enterprises were affected by the redevelopment: W. Jay (printer and lithographer) vacated his premises at 10 Castle Street, and G.T. Briant (pastry cook and confectioner) moved out of No. 12.

Castle Street, 1915. Nos 5 and 7 were occupied by Woodrow & Company, Ironmongers, and George Breeze was a newsagent and postcard seller at No. 9. In addition to managing her sweet and tobacco shop at No. 11, Mrs Sheppard ran a high-class registry office for servants. Next-door, at No. 13, William Graham was a corn and seed merchant. Also to be found along this side of the street was Harry Turpin's Sarum Toilet Saloon and Horace C. Messer's Photographic Studio.

Minster Street viewed from George Oliver's Boot Depot, 1908. Powney's Corner can be seen to the left, the site of Joseph Powney's boot and shoe shop. The Haunch of Venison is next-door, then W. Carter & Son (jewellers), Foster Brothers (outfitters), Misses Neale and Currie (refreshment rooms), Eastmans (butchers), Macey & Jeffrey (tobacconists), Stead & Simpson (footwear), and the London City and Midland Bank.

Butcher Row, 1906. Walter Hart invited custom by displaying cuts of meat on trestle-tables in front of his shop. Almost directly opposite Mrs Priscilla Hart was in business as a fishmonger and game dealer. The name Hart was synonymous with the Salisbury fish and meat retailing trades for more than one hundred years.

Queen Street, 1904. A Tuesday market is in progress. Immediately right is Jenkins (plumbers), followed by the Turkish Baths (manager, Harry Ponter), James Nelson & Sons (butchers), A.J. Chamberlain (gunsmith), Miss S. White (umbrella manufacturer) and Woodrow & Son (seedsmen). On the corner of Winchester Street Pinckney's branch of the Wilts and Dorset Banking Company could be found (Charles Southby was the resident clerk).

The Old Plume of Feathers Courtyard, 1939. The seventeenth-century staircase on the left can be seen today in the shopping mall known as Cross Keys Chequer. During the early years of this century it led to the Turkish Baths. Suspended above the exit to Queen Street is a sign advertising the services of Foley, Aylward and Spinney: 'Pianos, Accordeons [sic], Sheet Music and Records'.

The Council Chamber and Market Place in the nineteenth century. Planted at the time of Queen Victoria's Golden Jubilee in 1887, the lime trees depicted in the foreground have gone, as has the Sydney Herbert statue, which was removed to Victoria Park in the late 1950s. The tandem tricycle dates from around 1880.

Salisbury war memorial. Unveiled on 12 February 1922, the memorial is engraved with the following words: 'In Honour and Remembrance of the Citizens of Salisbury who Served. Who Fought. Who Died. For Freedom, Home and Humanity. 1914–1919.'

The Market Place, 1907. On Tuesday each week, over a period of many years, John Jeffery of Donhead St Mary held a sheep sale at Salisbury Market. On this particular day his four-wheeled auctioneer's booth was placed near the animal pens in the foreground. After twenty years of growth the trees around the square had only just reached first-floor level, giving an uninterrupted view of the upper storeys of the buildings along Oatmeal Row. Hancock Brothers (drapers and milliners), also Hilton's Booteries, Henry Neesham & Co. (cutlers), Brinsmead's Music Stores and the International Tea Warehouse (manager, Sidney Tambling). On the extreme right of the picture is New Sarum House, the trading place of W. Main & Sons (corn and seed merchants), now the offices of Annetts & Orchard Insurance and Portman Building Society.

A hundred years ago in Blue Boar Row. The illustration is taken from a very rare, if not unique, real photographic birthday card published by Richard Wilkinson of Trowbridge: 'May Health and Wealth and Happiness attend each Birthday.' The large emporium on the left was known as Style and Gerrish (established 1803), now Debenhams.

Pinder's Corner, 1916. In 1899 Joseph Edwin Pinder became joint proprietor of the Central Hardware Stores, which had been established on the corner of Endless Street and Winchester Street for around half a century. The business thrived by providing a good old-fashioned service, but times have changed, and in April 1987 the site was offered for sale.

Winchester Street, 1915. The YMCA Club Rooms can just be seen to the right, as well as the Soldier's Rest (manager, Fred Barge). On the other side of the street a number of properties were demolished and the site was cleared for the new Salisbury Co-operative Society building, which was opened in 1926. A McDonalds fast food outlet occupies the site now.

Endless Street, 1937. Nearest the camera is the original Woolpack inn (licensee, Charles Wigley), now the Wilts and Dorset Travel Office. The former waiting rooms and buffet of the Wilts & Dorset Motor Services were in the neighbouring building which now houses The Tavern Alehouse. At this time the old Invicta Leather Works (established 1824) were occupied by three concerns: W.S. Low (wallpaper merchants), Elders and Fyffes (fruit importers) and the offices of the Salisbury Divisional Labour Party (A.F. Soffe, hon. sec.). The Wilts and Dorset Leyland bus (formerly a Rowland's vehicle) appears to be operating on the Mere service. Some will remember it affectionately as the 'Coronation Coach'. Pinder's Corner can be seen at the far end.

The Palace Theatre, Endless Street, 1920s. Originally built as the County Hall, this fine Queen Anne style auditorium was opened on 16 September 1889. It changed hands twenty years later and became Albany Ward's Electric Variety Palace. Throughout the 1950s and 1960s it was the home of Palace Garages (English's) and soon after they moved out the building was demolished. Sarum Seeds are in business here today.

Salt Lane (formerly Cow Lane) 1937. When the Rollestone Street corner was cut back some years ago the old Cow Lane street sign was lost. The black letters on a white background are just visible. The fourteenth-century building which is now the Pheasant Inn was the Crispin Inn two hundred years ago and the Rainbow Inn in the 1800s.

The Greencroft, *c.* 1935. Len Viney is the young man wearing light-coloured trousers at the head of the queue. Also waiting to buy twopenny-halfpenny Eldorado ice cream wafers are Edna and Mary Burden, 'Sonny' Bundy, Don Conio, Les Jeans, Charlie Smith, George Stevens and Don Witt. Churchill Way runs through here today.

London Road, before the First World War. Nearest the camera is Percy Harrison (butcher), followed by Rogers & Frampton (cycle engineers), and William Burry, who is pictured in the doorway of his boot repair shop. The trees were cut down in the late 1960s, before Churchill Way was constructed. The thoroughfare is now Estcourt Road.

Wain-a-Long Road during the First World War. The dwelling immediately to the left is No. 17, originally known as Sheriton Lodge. From around the turn of the century until the 1970s only two families resided here: the Baglins and the Bamkins. In 1922 an unusual note was pencilled on the back of this original picture: 'Mrs Tryhorn is on her war path again.'

St Mark's Road, 1905. No cars. No people. No trees. Just houses. So peaceful. So different. A little way down on the left, at No. 15, Frank Chew had fixed a sign on the front of his house which read: 'Registered Plumber and Hot Water Engineer'. A similar sign can be seen across the road at No. 22: 'William Sutton, Plumber and Decorator'.

On Wheels

A southward-bound steam train pulling away from Salisbury in around 1906. The 4–4–0 engine is an 'Adams' class locomotive, No. 464. Churchill Way North and Castle Roundabout dominate much of this area today. Of the five Castle Road houses on the right, only Nos 18, 20 and 22 have survived; Nos 14 and 16 were demolished to make way for the roundabout.

Walter Clements' 'Xtraordinary'. Introduced in around 1870 and developed from the earlier Velocipede design, the ordinary bicycle was more commonly known as the penny farthing. In 1885 the Salisbury Cycling and Athletic Club was formed by a few local cyclists who enjoyed a weekly ride in the country.

A rare Phebus-Aster motor tricycle and trailer, purchased by Samuel Augustus Smith of 1 Radnor Terrace, Queen's Road, Salisbury, before December 1903. This unusual machine was manufactured in France around 1900. Mr Smith was proprietor of a music shop at 78 Fisherton Street, known as Handel House.

Charles Thomas Langford and Son, with AM 317, a 1903 Quadrant motorcycle. The shop which Mr Langford opened at 40 Winchester Street in around 1900 could still be found there twenty years later. By 1923, however, his cycle business had moved across the street to No. 57, where it survived until the mid-1950s.

A superior combination. Taken in the late 1920s at the North Gate of Victoria Park, our picture shows an 8 hp Brough Superior motorcycle and Montgomery side-car combination. On 26 July 1923 Wiltshire County Council allocated registration mark HR 9177 to S.J. Butt of 8 Bridge Street, Salisbury.

Tom with Charlie and the trap, at Fisherton in around 1912. Thomas Dowty, a Whaddon based builder, carpenter and undertaker, is pictured with Charlie his pony at the London & South Western Railway Station. They were the very best of friends.

A one-horse laundry wagon. The Salisbury Steam Laundry employed horse-drawn vehicles of several different types and each one was designed and constructed to best carry out its particular job. Known as the Town Tilt, this example has fixed body sides, a tail-gate and a canvas sheet covering the load platform. With small wheels fitted to the steering axle as shown, the van was very manoeuvrable and it could virtually be turned around on a six-pence. This ideal vehicle for the city roundsmen is waiting outside the laundry packing room in St Edmund's Church Street on 9 May 1914.

Opposite: A horse-drawn fly in Church Street, Fisherton, in around 1899. The cabman could well be William Kelloway of 7 Hillview Terrace, Milford Hill. His carriage stands outside Mill Cottages, in the thoroughfare known today as Mill Road. In the early 1930s the Mill Race Hotel was established here.

A Wiltshire wagon at work, 1910. In the distance more than twenty cattle vans can be seen moving along the London railway line, and in the top right hand corner you may just be able to make out the bell turret of St Andrew's church at Laverstock. An anonymous photographer took the picture from a field on the western side of London Road, now the Bishopdown housing estate.

William Thorn's sturdy farm wagon, in Castle Street, *c.* 1904. The team of four heavy horses had pulled the cart about six miles, from Church Farm at Durnford. Now owned by Post Office Counters Ltd, the ivy-covered house to the right was formerly the residence of Mr L.J. Parker, a dental surgeon.

Frederick Sutton's bread van, 1905. The side panels of this two-wheeled cart clearly advertise two of Mr Sutton's enterprises: a restaurant at 13 High Street and a bakery at 87 Crane Street. We do not recognize the roundsman.

Great Western Omnibus, VR 5786, which ferried railway passengers between the GWR station at Fisherton and various points around the city. The carriage was painted chocolate brown and cream, with gold leaf lettering, shadowed in crimson lake. The picture was taken before 1885.

A funeral carriage at the west front of Salisbury Cathedral. The deceased was Revd Edward King of Toronto who was tragically killed in a train crash above Fisherton Street Railway Bridge on 1 July 1906. He had travelled to England to attend a special service at St Paul's Cathedral, and after arriving safely at Plymouth on board the SS *New York* had joined the ill-fated Waterloo-bound express which sadly never reached its destination. A total of twenty-eight lives were lost. The hearse is believed to have been furnished by Frank Herring & Company of Fisherton Mews, 100 Fisherton Street.

Tea Rose, White Rose, or Royal Daylight. Throughout the United Kingdom horse-drawn bowsers like this collected lamp oil from the railway depots and delivered it to local factories, houses and shops. This Anglo-American Oil Company tanker was photographed on the old Southampton Road at around the time of the First World War.

A pair-horse landau in North Walk, c. 1900. It is thought that Harris & Sons of Winchester Street created this elegant canoe-styled carriage, a beautifully turned out example, which appears to be decorated for a wedding.

A Singer motor car at Edwards' High Street Garage, *c.* 1910. Arthur Edwards started out as a cycle dealer in the 1880s and opened his first shop at 48 New Street. His business flourished and by 1897 a second shop was taken on at 36 High Street (above). In 1905 a rather promising development took place when Singer & Company of Coventry began manufacturing motor cars and Edwards was offered the Salisbury franchise. A showroom and repair shop was quickly set up at 54–8 New Street, and additional workshops were acquired in Friary Lane. In 1947 the firm moved to its present site in Castle Street, formerly the Castle Garage. At about the same time they became authorized main dealers of Ford cars and commercials. Frank, Nana and Nip Edwards are pictured with a 16/20 hp French grey Singer rear-entry Tonneau, AM 1689.

Our past Member's Daimler in Endless Street. On 27 November 1906 Princess Christian came to Salisbury to open a YMCA bazaar at the County Hall. Her companion for the day was Lady Tennant, who can be seen arriving at the venue with her husband, Edward Priaulx Tennant, Member of Parliament for Salisbury.

Fine, fast and French. This attractive little car is a 1907 red and white painted two-seater manufactured by Gregoire et Cie of Poissy, Seine-et-Oise. The photograph was taken at Milford House, the residence of its owner, Mr Hubert Gale Ware of Ware Brothers Limited, leather merchants. The car carried registration mark AM 1156.

A green Charron laundaulette, 1912. Registered originally to W. Rowland & Sons, motor dealers of 102, 106 and 13 Castle Street, the car was sold to William Pepperell who ran it as a taxi. His taximeter can just be seen on the far side. The car looks very much like an early Renault with its radiator positioned behind the engine.

Blue Boar Row taxi-rank in the late 1920s. It appears from this scene that either the road was much wider at this time or motor cars were much smaller. Not only was this a line of taxis waiting for fares in the middle of the road, but there were also handcarts, private cars and delivery vehicles parked on both sides, and a two-way traffic system was operating.

The power of twenty horses under the bonnet. In August 1912 this blue-coloured 20 hp model-T Ford was registered to Mr Hamilton Fulton of The Corner House, The Close. Seven years later it was sold to Jane Mirfin, a taxi operator of 69A Brown Street.

Joseph Pinder, 1924. The hardware business founded by Joseph Edwin Pinder on the corner of Endless Street and Winchester Street in 1899 was finally wound up in around 1987. A fully qualified Expert and Fellow of the Royal Entomology Society, he is at the wheel of his Humber two-seater loaded with a hive and a container of live bees.

A motor ambulance at Salisbury Infirmary, 1916. Based on the Ford model-T chassis, the vehicle was equipped to transport four sitting and two stretchered patients, plus an attendant. The driver on this occasion was a soldier from 348 Company MT, RASC, Wilton.

Fred's Ford delivering bread and buns. It is thought that the roundsmen were photographed at Hanging Langford in 1925, while out on one of their regular runs through the Wylye Valley. By 1931 Fosters Bakery was at 65 Milford Street.

A motor hearse in Devizes Road, April 1939. The deceased was Sergeant Frederick George Harvey (aged 42) of the Salisbury City Police. His attendants were Sergeants Brewer, Cobden, Curtis and Syrett, and Constables Churchill and Hutchings. The Buick funeral cars were supplied by Albert Cheater, undertaker, of 57 Station Road, Romsey.

Tiny's Humber delivering haddock or hake. By 1915 Joseph Bowden's fish, poultry and game shop was well established at 27 Castle Street. Situated in a good position close to the main post office, the business survived well into the 1960s. Arthur 'Tiny' Bowden is pictured at Kingsbury Square, Wilton with the firm's 28 hp Humber van.

Walter's Willys in Salisbury Market Place, March 1921. This blue-coloured, 20 hp, Willys-Overland model-65 van was manufactured in Toledo, Ohio, USA in 1913. It was subsequently exported to the United Kingdom and sold to William Sainsbury, the Shrewton carrier. At the time of this photograph the vehicle was recorded in the Wiltshire hackney carriage register under the name of Walter Sainsbury. The body was specifically designed for a country carrier: removable bench seats were installed in the rear compartment (maximum fourteen persons) and a substantial roof-rack was fitted. It appears that the van boy had been sent off to collect brown-paper parcels from local shops, and he can be seen transferring them from the handcart to the van.

Watts' wartime wagons. Four of Ernest James Watts' ex-War Department Daimler army lorries stand in The Canal in the mid-1920s. The dark green 4 ton trucks appear to be loaded rather precariously with a number of dismantled army huts.

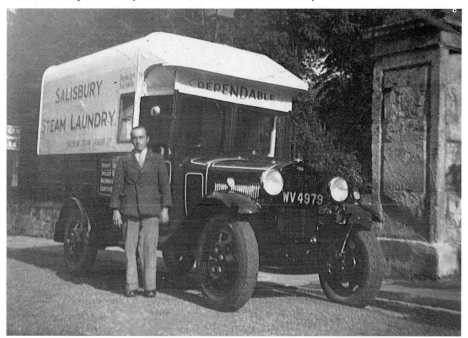

Dependable in blue and white. Mr Acton proudly stands alongside a handsome new Ford A type laundry van which had just been completed at his vehicle body works at 2 Greencroft Street. Finished in the blue and white livery of Salisbury Steam Laundry, WV 4979 was photographed outside the Bourne Hill Council House in April 1934.

A bonny Bedford. Anna Valley Motors of Castle Street supplied this appealing little Bedford ML 2/3 ton van to the Wessex Aircraft Engineering Company of Highpost. GMR 609 was licensed on 25 April 1950.

Commers were good old carriers. The earliest Commer commercial vehicles were made at Luton in 1905; four years before the first Scout industrial chassis was built in Salisbury. One of several local Commer agents during the early post-war years, Jack Miles Ltd of Harnham Garage, New Bridge Road, supplied MMW 806 to W. Main & Sons Ltd, the corn and seed merchants of New Sarum House. In the spring of 1955 a Commer 5 ton QX/80A chassis/cab was delivered to Hayden & Son of Netherhampton, who assembled and fitted this wood and metal body. The lorry was painted dark green with gold lettering and a tan-coloured tarpaulin protected the load platform. Harnham Garage now stands empty, a victim of the recession and the collapse of B.D. Amos, BMW agents, who had been trading here for some time.

Opposite: Beer in abundance during the Second World War. One of John Lampard's AEC Matadors was on hire to John Lovibond & Sons of St Ann's Brewery in around 1942. It regularly hauled barrels between the breweries at Salisbury and Greenwich. The driver's cab and the platform body were manufactured at Lee Motor Works in Wimborne Road, Winton. DRU 342 is a 1937 Bournemouth registration.

John Salter's first Foden steam lorry, a 1908 5 ton model, carrying a removal container for Case & Sons. A horse-drawn pantechnicon is hitched on behind. One can easily imagine the noise created by this heavy machine as it trundled along the road on bare metal wheels. The ride was improved somewhat on later models by the fitting of solid rubber tyres, as can be seen on the wagon below.

A later Foden at Salter's Yard, 100A Fisherton Street. Mr Salter was a refreshment contractor, who frequently used Foden 5 tonners to carry marquees and catering equipment around the Salisbury Plain military camps. He also managed the Bird-in-Hand Inn in North Street. The man standing on the extreme left is Charles Salter, one of John's three sons.

Celebration in steam, 1902. The photograph was taken in Brown Street near Henry Manner's hostelry, the Wagon & Horses Inn. Hardy & Son's warehouse was on the other side of the street, from where one of their traction engines has been decorated with flags, bunting and chinese lanterns in celebration of King Edward VII's coronation. Both Tasker & Sons of Andover, and Wallis & Steevens of Basingstoke had supplied Hardy & Son with steam wagons, but we are not quite sure which one is depicted here.

Charabanc visitors from afar, at the Pig Market in 1922. This smart AEC twenty-eight seater was No. 2008 in the National Omnibus Company fleet of Brompton Road, London. Formerly an army lorry, the vehicle was converted into a pleasure car after the First World War. Its military transport towing hooks and crash bar can still be seen on the front of the chassis.

Day-trippers at the Pig Market, 1924. Eleven adults and six youngsters squeezed into this tiny Ford model-T wagonnette. In contrast to the AEC charabanc above (with its six rows of padded seats) this conveyance just had two plain wooden benches, fitted longitudinally. The owner was S.J. Morris of 17 The Halve, Trowbridge. The Roe Buck Inn and George Bath's shop can be seen in the background.

This single-deck AEC bus was photographed for a motoring magazine feature in April 1921, exactly twelve months after it was supplied to Wilts & Dorset Motor Services. Powered by a 45 hp Tyler engine, the refurbished ex-military YC type chassis was fitted with a thirty-five seat rear-entrance bus body, manufactured by the Dodson coachbuilding company. It was given fleet No. 10. On the occasion of its first birthday the vehicle was covering Service 3, a regular run from Salisbury to Bournemouth via Fordingbridge and Ringwood, which had been inaugurated just a few weeks earlier.

A Lancashire lass in Ivy Street. Manufactured by Leyland Motors Limited, this handsome S5 charabanc was supplied to Wilts & Dorset Motor Services in May 1921. The original Harrington dual-entrance body (designed to carry thirty-three passengers plus the driver) did not remain on the chassis for very long, and by 1926 a new, locally manufactured replacement had been fitted. Six years later, in 1932, the vehicle was sold and converted into a lorry for John Lampard of West Harnham. Harry Rewse of Fisherton Street photographed this all-male party outside the Queen's Arms public house in around 1926.

Departing from Devizes Road, 1920s. The two charabancs outside H. Parsons' shop at 37 Devizes Road were operated by Hall's of Orcheston. The conveyance in the foreground is a Daimler CK type 26 seater, which was garaged at Orcheston. The second machine is a thirty-two seat AEC YC type from the Hindon garage.

Annual outing for the staff of Woodrow & Company, which took place before the Second World War. One of several pleasure cars hired for the occasion from W. Rowland & Sons, this is their Leyland No. 3. The man standing on the running-board, just left of centre, is Leslie Smith, who later became a coach driver. In 1936 Rowland & Sons was taken over by Wilts & Dorset Motor Services.

Double-decker on the St Mark's Church via Devizes Road service in the 1930s. Frederick Dredge and Charles Lucas stand in front of a Wilts and Dorset Leyland LT2 at the terminus near the junction of Roman Road with Coronation Road.

Buick, black and beautiful, 1922. This highly polished, black, sixteen seater charabanc body was assembled and fitted to a Buick chassis by the craftsmen at The Salisbury Carriage Works in Wilton Road. The business was taken over by Frank Readhead in 1922/3. The Southern Command offices, known as Evelyn House, can be seen to the right and Eton Terrace is to the left. The offices, however, have been demolished and Homesarum House is on the site today

The Bournemouth bus in Queen Street, 1921. This dark-green 40 hp Leyland was operated by Hants and Dorset Motor Services of the Royal Mews, Norwich Avenue, Bournemouth. Registered EL 5553 in November 1920, the vehicle became a familiar sight as it ran regular services from its Hampshire base through Christchurch and Ringwood to Salisbury. The passengers stepped down directly opposite No. 20 Queen Street, the premises of Woodrow & Son, corn, seed, cake, and manure merchants.

Country buses in the Market Place, 1921. Charles Haines's Durrington bus, a tiny Crossley charabanc, is visible in the extreme left hand corner. Next to it is the *Royal Red*, an AEC charabanc (HR 1397) operated by Frederick Rawlings of Hindon, who serviced the villages of Chilmark, Fonthill, Hindon and East Knoyle. *The Speedwell* is next in line, which we believe was driven by Walter Morgan. On Tuesday and Saturday each week this vehicle covered the Broughton to Salisbury route. The neighbouring space was occupied by the Martin and Sixpenny Handley conveyance, a Dennis saloon bus with fitted roof seats, owned by Cox and MacDonald. Edwin Cave's *Upavon Bus* is in the following bay; this too was a Dennis saloon. The strange looking machine in the distance (with a man leaning on its coal-scuttle front) is AM 7821, a yellow and maroon coloured Austin, operated by Cecil Martin Wort of Bishopstone. The two most distant vehicles are an AEC and a Scout from Hall's Orcheston garage.

SECTION FIVE

At Your Service

Service with a smile from Ivy Street Dairy in the 1930s. Harry Oates stands on the corner of Albany Road with his faithful old chum Budge. Throughout the 1930s and '40s, man, dog and three-wheeled dairy pram were a familiar sight around the city. They were based at 12 Ivy Street.

Alfred John Elliott (1860–1912), in the sitting room of his Castle Street home. In 1901 he acquired the long-established pleasure boat and wholesale grocery businesses which a few benevolent individuals originally set up for Edmund Found (a foundling who was discovered abandoned at St Edmund's church after being deserted by his mother). The pleasure boats were operated from 6 Avon View and the grocery supply business was run from 91 Castle Street.

Elliott's pleasure boats, *c.* 1910. Percy Harold Elliott became proprietor of the firm when his father died in 1912, although from 1945 onwards the everyday running of the business was undertaken by his daughter Beryl, assisted by her husband, Basil Gerald Wainwright. In around 1964 the boathouse and all but one of the boats were sold to Salisbury Council.

Charles Henry Baker (1868–1950), founder of the well known Salisbury outfitters, known as Chas H. Baker. Born in Bath, he moved to Salisbury and in 1902 purchased Miss Sarah Ann Short's tailoring business at 15 Milford Street. Charles 'Reginald' Baker took over from his father in 1946 and ten years later doubled the shop frontage by purchasing No. 17 (Jesse Denham's Bakery). Celebrating the firm's ninetieth anniversary in 1992 is the founder's grandson and present proprietor, Robert Baker.

Coronation decorations, 1937. Left to right: Frank Ambrose (an employee for fifty-one years), -?-, Charles Henry Baker, David Baker (founder's grandson), Reginald Baker, Mr Parsons. Reginald died in 1986 while doing something he really enjoyed: working at the shop. He passed away in his office, just 20 feet from the spot where he was born eighty-two years previously.

Henry Job Sutton (1854–1935). Born in Salisbury, he lived in the Mill House, St Thomas's Square (now Snell's) with his wife Artula (née Cook Spear), whom he married in London in 1884. For a relatively short time he ran the town mill and then, in 1896, following a couple of years working Wylye Mill, he bought an acre of land just off the Southampton Road, where he built the Waterloo Steam Roller Flour Mills.

Waterloo Flour Mills, employees and vehicles. Depicted in the right foreground is one of the first Foden steam lorries to be used in the city (M 2321). The plant was taken over by Ranks in 1929 and Henry and Artula moved to Parkstone, Dorset where they bought a bakery. The building is now the Tintometer factory.

Sydney George Best (1884–1949). A pupil of St Thomas's School, he later trained as an accountant with Keith Dowden (mayor of Salisbury, 1904) at Bank Chambers. Just before leaving for the Middle East in 1917 he married Emily Penfound at St Mary's church, Portsea. Following his return from the First World War, and the retirement of Mr Dowden, he opened an office at 31 Castle Street (formerly Cox & Son, saddlers). Later he became a prominent auctioneer with sale-rooms in Brown Street, and during the Second World War he organized numerous concerts at the Guildhall.

Best & Cox and Eastman's. When this photograph was taken in around 1957 Philip Eastman had decided to retire and the shop which he had occupied at 29 Castle Street since 1920 was to close. The premises had been in the hands of commercial photographers since 1891, originally John Arney & Son (Victoria Studio), then Horace C. Messer, from 1896 to 1920.

Vincent James Blew. Born in Bristol in 1851, he moved to Salisbury before 1880 and set himself up as a removal contractor, coal merchant and Great Western Railway parcel agent, with offices at 23 Milford Street. He lived at 13 Osborne Terrace, Windsor Road. An early member of the Salvation Army Salisbury City Band, he is pictured here wearing a smart braided tunic. In 1912 he emigrated to Canada, where he worked as an accountant. His wife Harriet (neé Harris), whom he married at Bristol in 1876, and his two youngest daughters followed on a short time later. He died in Calgary, Alberta in 1929.

Blew's boys moving Brown's belongings, 1910. Their Swiss-made petrol-engined Orion removal van stands outside George Brown's house at 12 Hulse Road. The new occupier was Edwin Barnett (tailor), who was in residence for only a short time when the house numbers were changed and No. 12 became No. 34.

'Not Mould, or Mole, or Moles, but Mold!' Throughout the 1920s, '30s and '40s the brothers Mold could be seen and heard on the streets of Salisbury as they toured around entertaining shoppers with this fine Pasquale street piano. Despite the fact that they were handicapped and unable to work the three brothers were given the opportunity to earn a respectable living through the kindness of a few friendly people who provided them with this wheeled instrument. There were eleven children in the family altogether: Charlie (in gents service), Alf (steward on the White Star liner *Adriatic*), Willie, Teddy, Sammy (left), Harry, Bertie, Emma, Elizabeth (missionary), Nellie and Elsie. The family home was at 24 Ashley Road. In November 1908, because of his association with Mrs Flora Fanny Haskell of 40 Meadow Road, Alf was interviewed by Mr Frank Richardson, Chief Constable of Salisbury, and Chief Inspector Walter Drew of Scotland Yard, in connection with the murder of Teddy Haskell (see page 128). The investigators were soon convinced that he was not involved, however, and no further action was taken.

Fresh produce weekly. When set up in 1932, the Women's Institute stall at Salisbury Market was the first of its kind in Wiltshire, and only the fifth in England. Mrs Gulliver of Elm Farm, Nunton and Mrs Hill can be seen among the women in this group.

Salisbury October Fair in 1905, from the roof of the Market House (now Salisbury Library). Doomer's Electrograph can be seen facing the camera, 'Always to the Fore at Events'. The large tent in the foreground may well have contained McKeowen's boxing ring.

Jeffery's Winchester Street Tobacco Stores, 1902. Situated on the corner of St Edmund's Church Street and Winchester Street, the business was founded by Walter Henry Jeffery before 1890. It survived for around eighty years and finally closed down in 1968/9. The shop was decorated on this occasion for the coronation of Edward VII in August 1902. A few familiar-sounding products can be seen displayed here among the crowns, the flags and the ribbons: Ogden's 'Guinea Gold Cigarettes', Will's high-class tobacco and Player's 'Navy Mixture'. Alpha Gallery can be found here today.

Thomas Bloom's shop on the corner of New Canal and Catherine Street, 1887 or 1897. Among the first concerns in the city to use Alexander Graham Bell's invention, the shop was allocated telephone number 7. Benetton are here now.

The New Canal smithy. Founded in around 1879 by Henry Paul Pollard, in 1910 the business was sold to Frederick William Armstead (proprietor of a Newton Toney blacksmith's shop). Stephen Meaden of Imber is the farrier shoeing a horse at the time of the First World War. The site is now occupied by the Galleon Café.

Bentlif's Brush Manufactory, 1897. Situated at 7 Winchester Street, the business was founded by Philip Bentlif in around 1878. By 1908 George Kington was the proprietor. This picture was taken as a souvenir of Queen Victoria's Diamond Jubilee, when the building was adorned with flags. On the extreme left one can see the entrance to Three Swans Yard and Harding's livery and bait stables.

Left: Victoria Temperance Hotel and Coffee Tavern. The business which William Collins started at 13 Butcher Row in around 1895 had been sold to George Coombes by 1903. The woman pictured in the doorway is Amy Coombes, the proprietor's sister. A branch of Milwards Shoes can be found here today.

Below: Wiltons Ironmongers on New Canal, 1935. A stock clearance sale was being held prior to the firm's move to 71–3 Castle Street (previously the New Theatre). The Salisbury Electric Light and Supply Company vacated their premises at 27 Market Place to move to this site.

John Wilkes & Son, Ironmongers, 1865. For almost a hundred years the name Wilkes could be seen above the door of the shop on the corner of Milford Street and Queen Street. By 1931, however, the firm had gone and the premises were occupied by the Salisbury Co-operative Society furnishing showrooms. In September 1937 the building was seriously damaged by fire.

Radio Services, c. 1937. Situated next to Three Swans Yard in Winchester Street, Mr Sidney Chalk (mayor of Salisbury, 1951) was the proprietor. Pictured here with a consignment of new HMV radios are Bill Daniels (not related to the author), Archie Cambell, Eddie Chalk (not related to the proprietor), Ewart Garrett, Sidney Locke and Myles Tibbetts. Frank Ray was the driver of the GWR lorry.

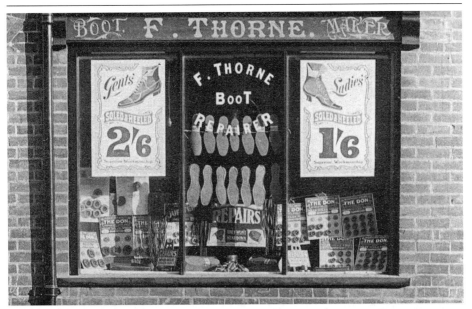

'Ladies' and Gents' Soled and Heeled,' 1909. Frederick Thorne occupied this shop at 110 Castle Street for just a few months. Labourer William Eyres was living here in 1908 and by 1910 boot-maker Albert Hoole was in residence.

G.W. Rouse, Baker and Confectioner. Employed for a number of years by Frederick Sutton, George Walter Rouse resigned in around 1900 and set up his own bakery at 65 Castle Street. Several other names have been seen above the shop window since then: J. Woodford by 1914, F. Nicholas by 1920 and S. Appleby from around 1930 to the present day.

Anna Valley Motors, 1950s. Successors to W. Rowland & Sons in 1936, the firm operated here until 1 August 1973, when it was removed to Churchfields Industrial Estate. Charlie Smith was the petrol pump attendant for most of that time and he can be seen here directing Mr A.F. Alexander and his Vauxhall saloon (KAM 119) safely off the forecourt.

W. Rowland & Sons cycle engineers at 13 Castle Street. Opened by 1899, the shop was vacated before 1913 when the business was transferred to the firm's newly built garage and workshops at 102–06 Castle Street (formerly ten dwellings known as Newmans Court). For many years the company operated a large fleet of charabancs and hire cars.

Harris & Son carriage builders and motor engineers, early 1920s. Founded in The Canal by John Harris in 1836, the business later moved to 20–2 Winchester Street (formerly the Black Horse Inn), where it remained until after the Second World War. Ernest Lampard is second from right.

Burdens General Store at 69 St Ann Street, 1930s. During the early years of the twentieth century Mrs Brockway lived here; by 1920 it was the residence of Mr and Mrs Alfred Thomas Burden. Some building alterations had been carried out by 1927 and Mrs Burden was running a small general store, while her husband continued working as a chimney sweep. The last occupier was Ernest Sims, who moved out in around 1968 prior to the construction of the Churchill Way East pedestrian subway entrance which occupies the site today. On the right of the picture is the passage to Payne's Hill, through which the author walked many times in the 1950s while going to and from St Martin's Infant School.

St Ann Street post office, 1920s. Originally opened as a grocery store and bakery in around 1896, William Prince was selling stationery and stamps on the premises by 1907. Having survived two world wars and several depressions it seems a great pity that business had to cease in June 1992. 'Profit before people' is an aphorism of our modern age.

Elizabeth Harfitt at her Iron, Zinc & Tin Plateworks, 1905. Frederick Harfitt had been carrying on the trade of a tinsmith in Salt Lane since before 1880, but by 1904 Elizabeth (born 1870) was running the company. From around 1922 until 1972, Elizabeth's son Frank was manufacturing and selling baby carriages here. This is now Buddies Restaurant.

Culver Street Grocery Store, before 1920. M. Albert Dear started trading at 78 Culver Street in around 1906, but by 1915 he had sold the business to Thomas Stone (the tall man pictured here in the doorway?) and the shop was extended, taking in No. 80. The passage leading to Spring Place can be seen on the extreme left.

Wyndham Hotel, London Road, 1906. Established well over a hundred years ago, the hostelry is now known as the Wyndham Arms. Nellie Matilda House was the resident housemaid at this time and she can be seen standing in the doorway in College Street. Her employer was William Wise (licensee from around 1894 to 1906).

Southampton Road Clock Manufactory, 1905. During the closing years of the last century Moore Bros & Co. were manufacturing boots and shoes here, but by 1903 it was known as the English Clock Factory (H. Williamson Ltd, proprietors). In the distance we can see The Laurells, the residence of George Bley, the works manager. The factory was destroyed by fire in May 1909.

SECTION SIX

People

Plum pudding and ginger pop, 1911. This is not a record of some strange ritual being performed, but simply a souvenir picture of a group of local men who had gathered in the Market Place to enjoy a midday feast in celebration of King George V's coronation. Included in the crowd are Mr Palmer (railway detective), Mr Safe (builder's labourer), the brothers Dee, Mr Gaisford (rifle volunteer), Mr Say (rifle volunteer), Walter Garrett and Mr Nelmes.

Stanley Pittman, 'Old Sarum Archer'. In June 1927 over three thousand school children took part in a street procession to celebrate 'Seven Hundred Years of Salisbury'. Each school group portrayed a different period of the city's past. Stanley (aged ten) joined fellow pupils of St Paul's Boys' School who dressed up as Old Sarum Archers (bow and arrow society members who practised below Old Sarum during the late 1700s). Also taking part was schoolgirl Edna Carnell from the Highbury Avenue Council School, who later became Stanley's wife.

Ron Percy and his New Swing Band, 1940s. The band leader is standing third from the left, next to the drums, and Charlie Overton is on the right. In the centre of the group is Claude Nineham, a piano tuner who moved to Salisbury from Bournemouth in the mid-thirties. He worked for Sam Smith at Handel House in Fisherton Street.

Connie Sutton, a nurse at Salisbury Infirmary, from a photograph taken by her husband in the 1920s. The photographic studio which Stanley Sutton opened at 45 The Canal in around 1919 could still be found there in the mid-forties. Formerly residing at 9 Canadian Avenue, by the mid-thirties the couple had moved to a new home at 43 Cornwall Road, known as Waylen. They were still living there in the early fifties. Connie's husband will also be rememberd as an organist at the Salisbury Infirmary chapel.

College girls at Barnard's Cross. On 18 October 1908 this picture postcard view of the Salisbury Training College was sent to Miss Nobbs of Frome St Quintin, Cattistock, Dorset: 'Dear Madge, I'm coming home next Saturday for a week (hip hip), shall hope to see you then. I have a bad cold and Miss Allen wouldn't kiss me when she put out our lights because I sounded so microbish.' Rosie Waspfield was the sender.

A junior usher at the Gaumont Palace, 1931. Born on 23 January 1917, Ernest Frank was the third son of Edward 'John' Amps and Nellie 'Matilda', (née House, former maid at the Wyndham Hotel, see page 116). Ern's brothers were named Ted (eldest), Fred (presently residing at Bishopdown) and Ron. The family lived at No. 1 Maton Gardens, Bedwin Street. The junior usher's post at the new Gaumont Palace cinema (now the Odeon) was Ern's first regular job.

The marriage of Archie Sanger and Edith Bath. Left to right: Mrs Sanger (her husband James ran the bone-crushing mill at West Harnham, now the Old Mill), Phyllis Sanger (groom's sister), Archie Sanger, Miss Edith Bath, Harry Sanger (groom's brother), Mrs Bath, George Bath (proprietor of several Salisbury butchers shops), Miss Dorothy Bath (bride's sister).

Salisbury telegraph boy number five. Herbert 'Bert' Larcombe can be seen here in F. Futcher & Son's studio at 19 Fisherton Street. The son of a railway guard, he lived at 2 Kingsland Road.

Auntie Smiler and friends, 1935. Assembled by the staff of Salisbury Steam Laundry for the Hospital Carnival of 1930, the mechanical giantess here in Blue Boar Row was taking part in her second major appearance: The King George V Silver Jubilee Parade. Joe Bunsell and Jack Tilley pulled her all the way to Victoria Park.

Liberal Member of Parliament for Salisbury in 1906, the Right Honourable Edward Priaulx Tennant. Born in 1859, he was the son of Sir Charles Tennant, Baronet. During the early years of the twentieth century he lived at Wilsford Manor House. Educated at Eton and Trinity College, Cambridge he was a merchant in the City of London, a former Secretary to Sir George O. Trevelyan and a member of Wiltshire County Council.

The Mayor and councillors of Salisbury, March 1918. The gentlemen were photographed in the Market Place, beside a First World War battle tank (No. 211) which was the focus of everyone's attention during War Bond Week. The cumbersome contraption was paraded around the city streets. The Mayor, Sir James Macklin is in the middle of the group and councillor F.W. Wort is on the left, walking stick in hand.

Conservative Member of Parliament for Salisbury in 1910, the Right Honourable Godfrey Locker-Lampson, who for a number of years lived at Harnwood House, Old Blandford Road, East Harnham. The result of the general election of January 1910 was as follows: Conservatives, 1803 votes; Liberals, 1485 votes, giving a Conservative majority of 318. In December 1910 another election was held and the Conservative majority in Salisbury was increased to 337.

A royal proclamation, 1910. This large crowd had gathered outside Stevens & Company's tobacco manufactory in Silver Street to hear the town clerk, Francis Hodding, announce the accession to the throne of King George V. His performance was repeated at numerous other sites around the city. The shop in the background on the right is now Thorntons.

Janitor Jim of Victoria Hall, 1920s. Employed for a number of years by Salisbury Swimming Baths Ltd and Salisbury Steam Laundry, James Hill was a busy man whose work very much depended upon the season of the year. For six months he could be seen wearing this uniform as he performed the duties of a concert-hall caretaker (the VH monograms are just visible on his collar); then, from 15 April to 15 October, he was janitor of Salisbury's only indoor swimming pool. The dance floor of the Rollestone Street hall was removable and every spring it was taken up section by section to reveal beneath it an 80ft x 40ft swimming bath.

Railway accident investigators, 1906. The detectives, inspectors, labourers and porters at the L&SWR Station are sifting through debris for clues and personal effects in the wake of Salisbury's worst ever rail crash. Twenty-eight lives were lost when a Waterloo-bound express smashed into a stationary engine near Fisherton Bridge.

Frederick Charles Feltham. Proud to be wearing his First World War soldier's uniform, 'Chas' is pictured here in the garden of the family home at 20 The Greencroft. Born the son of a tailor in 1898, he was named after his father. Much of his working life was spent at Woodrow & Company in Castle Street, where he was a senior member of staff in the brush department. He died in 1985.

Their country needed them. In September 1914 these brave young men left Salisbury by train to join Kitchener's army. All from very different backgrounds they included plasterers, plumbers, postmen and a publican; the latter, Herbert Bundy (under the arrow), gave up the tenancy of the London Road Inn (now known as the Winchester Gate). Some of the lads never came home.

Lords, ladies and the lads, April 1906. Field Marshal Lord Roberts officially opens a new shooting range for the Salisbury and District Rifle Club in the pleasure gardens behind the Market House (now the Public Library). The dean and his wife are to the left of the group, Lady Radnor and the Mayoress are nearer the centre, and Lord Radnor is to the right, wearing his 1st Wilts VRC uniform.

Bishop, brewer and butter man. Bishop Wordsworth can be seen presenting an award to the winner of a swimming contest at the old open-air baths off Fisherton Street (now The Maltings shopping precinct). Sitting beside him is the butter man, Tom Perkins of the South Wilts Dairy Company. John Folliot of the Old George Brewery is standing on the extreme right of the group; he was Mayor of Salisbury in 1902.

The Giant, Hob-nob, Whifflers and Grotesques. On 6 July 1893 Salisbury people cele-brated the marriage of the Duke of York and Princess Mary of Teck. Throughout the day numerous entertaining events took place, the most popular of which was the colourful parade which attracted more than seven thousand spectators. Putting in one of their infre-quent appearances, St Christopher and his entourage are pictured near Snook's Corner at the northern end of the High Street. A full programme of dancing and sports followed at Victoria Park and in the evening the 1st Wilts Rifle Volunteers headed a torchlight proces-sion down Castle Street and through the city to the Greencroft, where a large crowd had gathered to see the day's festivities brought to a close with a brilliant firework display.

Murdered schoolboy, Edwin Richard Haskell, known to everyone as Teddy. A happy, winning child, he lived with his devoted mother, Flora Fanny Haskell at 40 Meadow Road. His father died of consumption in 1902. Despite only having one good leg (his right limb was amputated below the knee as a result of bone disease) the youngster was surprisingly agile and a remarkably good footballer. On Saturday 31 October 1908, while sleeping in his bed, the twelve year old was murdered with a kitchen knife. His mother was charged with the crime but, after being twice tried for the felonious and wilful killing of her son, was found not guilty due to insufficient evidence. The case remains unsolved.

Teddy Haskell's grave, in Devizes Road Cemetery. A tender tribute from the directors of Salisbury Football Club can just be seen: a football made of small white flowers and purple violets with the words 'In Loving Memory'. Another pretty wreath was for 'Darling Little Teddy from his Loving Mother and Grandma'.

SECTION SEVEN

Poultry Cross to St Paul's

Poultry Cross and Silver Street, before 1870. Very few thoroughfares in the city were sur-faced at this time, although the area around the Poultry Cross had been metalled and stone-set pavements laid at the principal crossing-points and central road junctions. In the far distance is the High Street outlet of druggist Thomas Barber, which was demolished to make way for the building presently occupied by Barclays Bank. The new structure was completed in 1872 for Richardson Brothers (wine and spirit merchants) of Gigant Street.

Poultry Cross, 1906. On the right, at Nos 37–41 Silver Street, are the local branches of Charles Haskins (clothier), George Oliver (footwear supplier) and Thomas Lipton (provisions). Charles Haskins was also proprietor of the three-storey shop which can be seen behind the Poultry Cross, on the corner of Butcher Row. His business was advertised as 'The People's China and Glass Stores'.

Lipton's local branch, 1912. This was situated at 41 Silver Street from around 1895 until the mid-1960s. Third from the right is William Henry Orman, who was branch manager at the time. The cashier, Dora Yeates can be seen standing to the left in the shop entrance.

Greetings from the Colonial and American Fresh Meat Stores. For many years W. & R. Fletcher ran two butchers shops in Salisbury. The manager of the Silver Street branch was George Chandler, standing in the shop doorway just before Christmas 1912. Harold Newman is second from the left. The smaller outlet was situated at 147 Fisherton Street.

Robert Stokes' Tea, Coffee, Sugar and Fruit Stores, 1896. When Francis Stokes established his business at 53 Silver Street in 1776 he probably never thought that it would still be around some two hundred years later.

Robert Stokes' shop interior, after the Second World War. The cooked meat section can be seen on the right, nearest the camera, with the butter and cheese displays beyond; the grocery counters are to the left. Looking out through the front windows one can see Freeman, Hardy and Willis' shoe shop at 44 Silver Street.

Café Nicholas at 44 Silver Street, 1930s. A really enjoyable cup of tea was served here and their cakes and pastries were delicious. The Nicholas brothers were busy people: in addition to the tea rooms pictured above they ran a grocery shop, a post office and a bakery and confectionary at 25–7 Wilton Road.

Silver Street on market day, 1904. On the extreme left, at No. 50, is Charles Rawlings' outfitters shop. The Maypole Dairy Company was at No. 48 and Algernon Smee (bookseller, stationer and newsagent) was at No. 46. John Smeeth (parcel agent of 6 Windsor Road) is approaching in his horse-drawn wagon.

Snook's Corner. F.W. Woolworth's can just be seen on the extreme left, next to the Old House, which was occupied at the time by Haywards Jewellers. W.J. Snook & Company vacated their corner shop in the mid-1930s, and in 1939 the building was demolished.

The Shoulder of Mutton was in Bridge Street for over 250 years (licensed as an alehouse in 1742). Samuel Naish was landlord for a time in the middle of the nineteenth century; by the 1890s Thomas Wade was the hotel manager. Throughout the inter-war years Clifford Jones was the licensee. The building was demolished in 1962.

A carnival crowd in Bridge Street, 20 June 1906. Salisbury people turned out in their thousands to enjoy the first Hospital Carnival procession. The picture was taken from the Shoulder of Mutton Inn. We can see from the shop signs that Thomas Butt's fruitery and Mrs Martin's Tofferies were situated here.

The earliest known view of Bridge Street, photographed over a hundred years ago. Thomas Davis's shop on the right displays a wide selection of goods, including calendars, cigars and carte-de-visite photographs. On the other side of the street are the King's Head Hotel (D. Parker, manager), Goslett and Company (coal merchants), M. Sheppard (basket-maker) and the King's Head Brewery (A.D. Stroyan, manager). Following the construction of Fisherton Clock Tower in 1893 the buildings depicted to the left were demolished and work began on the County Hotel, which was completed by June 1895.

The town mill. In 1887 Mayor 'Fred' Griffin planted a commemorative tree on the peninsula in front of the mill and at the inauguration ceremony a glass bottle was buried under its roots, in which were placed a few old coins and an antique parchment note. When the Maltings site was redeveloped a few years ago 'The Jubilee Tree' was disturbed, but as far as we know the time capsule was not found.

County Hotel, 1905. 'Patronised by Royalty, the Chief Military Officers, and County Families. Up-to-date in every respect. Officially appointed Hotel to the Royal Automobile Club. Motor Union, Automobile Association, Road Club and Auto-Cycle Union. The largest Hotel in Wiltshire.'

The Clock Tower was presented to the city by Dr John Roberts in memory of his beloved wife Arabella. Our picture also shows that by 1904 a two-storey public convenience had been built near to its base; 'Ladies' at street level and 'Gentlemen' underground. Two years later a second structure was added, the upper part of which was fitted out as a cab-men's bothy. This was similar in design to the first unit, and situated adjacent to it.

The Infirmary, 1906. At this time the daily average number of in-patients was seventy-four and the total number of out-patients admitted during the year was 2,396. A lift was installed and some improvements were carried out in the operating ward. The first Hospital Carnival also took place that year.

An Edwardian view of Fisherton Street. The stone-paved area on the left was maintained for the horse-drawn cabs which parked there while waiting for fares. The entrance to the YWCA rooms, the Star of Hope Temperance Hotel and Wells Brothers' gas-powered printing works are on the right.

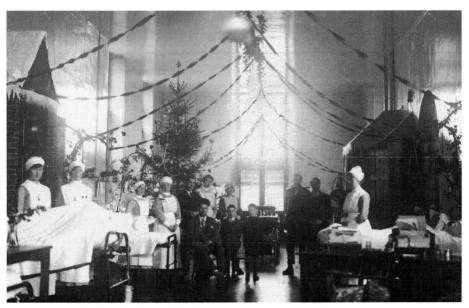

Christmas in Bartlett Ward, Salisbury Infirmary, 1924. The following names have been pencilled on the back of this original photograph: Bowler, Marchant, Wise and Youliston. It is not clear, however, if these refer to the nurses or their patients.

Fisherton Street in the snow. On 25 April 1908 a violent storm raged across southern England. The snowflakes that fell over Wiltshire were the largest that many people had ever seen, and for twelve hours or more they were blown and swept around by a menacing wind. Deep drifts built up on the outskirts of Salisbury and for some time the city was cut off from the rest of the county. It was an awe-inspiring sight and nothing like it had been experienced since the great storm of January 1881. Photographers turned out in large numbers to take pictures of the wintery scenes. This super example was taken by Frederick Futcher of 19 Fisherton Street.

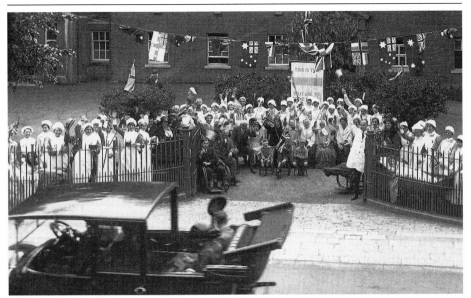

Red, white and blue, but mostly white. On 23 May 1923 the Prince of Wales came to Salisbury to open the annual show for the Wiltshire Agricultural Association, which on this occasion was held at the Butts Fair Field. He was driven from the station to the Council Chamber in an open Rolls Royce, which can be seen passing the Infirmary.

RAOB church parade, 30 August 1935. The Salisbury Province of the Royal Antediluvian Order of Buffaloes, and kindred societies, attended a thanksgiving service at the Cathedral in celebration of the Silver Jubilee. Our picture shows a group of nurses and VAD members joining the parade outside the Infirmary.

The Salisbury Giant in procession, 22 June 1911. The carnival cavalcade was part of an impressive programme of events held in celebration of the coronation of King George V. The giant can be seen trundling past the Congregational church on its way to the Market Place, which had been laid out with trestle-tables and benches for the menfolk of the city who took part in a midday feast. Following on behind is the Fisherton Conservative Club car, 'Britannia and Great Britain', The City Silver Spoon and Stewards, The Oddfellows' car, 'The Harvest of 100 Years', The Oddfellows' banner (New Sarum Lodge), and The Salvation Army Band.

A busy day in 1906. The vehicle depicted in the foreground appears to be a gardener's handcart. A timber panel is being carried (for a shed perhaps?), also a watering can, a sieve, a metal bucket and numerous other implements. Beyond that, to the right, a timber cart can be seen turning in to the yard of F.E. Hale (coal and builders' merchants).

Boating, but not for pleasure, 1915. Tom Perkins is the white-bearded man standing in the back of the skiff. He was manager of the South Wilts Dairy shop, which can be seen in the background. In 1909 he was Mayor of Salisbury. (For more about the flood see page 147.)

Fisherton Street post office and cash drug stores, 1912. The business was founded by Joseph Painter Harrison before 1875 and it survived until the 1920s, when it was taken over by Boots Cash Chemists. At some time F.J. Harrison (Joseph's son) acquired the neighbouring property, The Eagle Inn (Frank Penny, proprietor), and the business was enlarged. Left to right, in front of the original shop: M. Mountford, John Davidson, Douglas Biss, George Birss.

Charlotte Chapman's shop. No. 37 was a busy place where people queued quietly for quantities of paints, pencils, pictures, pigments, placards, postcards, posters, prints and puzzles; they rarely forgot their Ps and Qs. By 1908 Charlotte had moved her business up the road to No. 101.

When the world was at war. The imposing façade of Howard Lapham's Magnet Stores is on the right. Purchasers of bedsteads, brushes, mail carts, or even sheets of corrugated iron needed cash, as Mr Lapham gave no credit: 'Ready Money Only. Goods Must Be Paid For Before Delivery.'

John Raindle's butchers shop, 1910. Situated at No. 58 Fisherton Street, the business was founded in around 1880 and traded until the early 1930s. The carcasses pictured here are described as 'Prime Devon Ox Beef', several of which appear to be reserved: 'This Bullock has been Subscribed For by a Few Friends for the Poor of this City.'

Inspectors at Raindle's slaughterhouse, c. 1910. A large proportion of the meat purchased from Raindle's came from animals that were killed in their own licensed slaughterhouse, which was situated at the rear of the shop.

Fisherton Street in the flood, 1915. Following a sustained spell of heavy rain in early January the rivers Avon and Nadder overflowed and millions of gallons of water poured into Fisherton, Harnham and The Close. The water in this part of Fisherton Street was more than fourteen inches deep. Percy Elliott came to help out in one of the rowing boats which would ordinarily have been hired out for pleasure trips up the River Avon from the Castle Street Boathouse. He can be seen here near Jimmy Herring's horse-drawn phaeton and Chaplin & Company's delivery wagon.

The Angel YMCA. Situated at 66 Fisherton Street and known formerly as The Angel Hotel, the building was acquired for the purposes of extending the good work carried out at the Association's Winchester Street premises. Designated 'The Dunn Memorial' the refurbished hotel was reopened in April 1918.

Alfred Godwin (1858–1952), property owner, money lender, founder of a tannery and grindery at 73 Endless Street (*c.* 1895) and proprietor of a currier's shop at 61 Fisherton Street, which was opened before 1908. Two years later his retail business was extended with the acquisition of No. 59 (formerly occupied by gas-fitter Frederick Eynon). In due course Alfred retired and his three sons ran the business: Edgar and Walter controlled the Salisbury shops and Percy managed the branch at Trowbridge. From around 1935 until 1979 Edgar's son, Denis was looking after things and the founder's great-grandson, Roger Godwin is now the proprietor.

Godwin's and Snell's, dressed for the King, 21 June 1911. Charles Snell started trading as a fruiterer at No. 63, following 'Ernie' Longman's move to his new cycle depot at 97 Fisherton Street. The shops were decorated in celebration of King George V's coronation.

A backward glance, 1904. On the right hand side of the road, at Nos 65 and 67, are Bill Osmund's Refreshment Rooms and Tom Bridle's Haircutting and Shaving Salon. On the left, nearest the camera, is the Public Benefit Boot Company and Elias Baker's Cash Clothing Stores, of which more can be seen on page 152.

Chapman's Stores & Colonial Produce Merchant, 1908. William Chapman founded this business at 102 Fisherton Street in around 1899 and it survived well into the 1940s. Fung Ting Chinese Take Away is now here.

Fisherton Street under water, 24 February 1883. Although not quite as deep as the flood of January 1915, this deluge was the cause of much misery to the shopkeepers and residents of this busy street. A cellar wall at the Infirmary also had to be hurriedly shored up when it started to collapse under the pressure of the water.

The boys followed the band. It is thought that these are men of the 2nd Battalion, Wiltshire Regiment, who were invited to Salisbury on 7 September 1907. Upon their arrival at the Market House, and in the company of the Mayor and Corporation, nineteen officers and 422 men were each given a hot meal and a souvenir postcard.

Limelight Lanterns & Slides, 1915. These words appear in the top right hand corner of the picture, on the swinging sign attached to the Cash Clothing Stores. A contemporary advertisement for the firm highlighted their value-for-money clothing: 'Made-to-Measure Trousers from 7s 6d, and Quality Tweed Suits from 25s 6d'. The proprietor was Elias Baker, the pioneer of cinematography in Salisbury and a very well known presenter of 'Magic Lantern' slide shows. He died on the day of the Children's Peace Pageant, 28 July 1919, at the age of 77. On the left of the picture H. Case & Sons' horse-drawn delivery wagon (their premises were at 26 Water Lane) stands outside W. Sutton & Co.'s bakery.

Brittan & Son, Waterloo Nursery, 1907. John Brittan established himself as a gardener and seedsman at 49 High Street before 1842, and by 1885 his son had opened a fruit and flower shop at 122–4 Fisherton Street. Above, in the shop doorway, is Edward John Brittan (mayor of Salisbury, 1902). The company was taken over by William Gullick in 1912.

Fisherton Cycle Depot, 1911. Ernest James Longman is astride the Bedfordshire motor-cycle, BM 1064. He started manufacturing cycles in around 1895, initially at No. 63 Fisherton Street (formerly the *Western Gazette* offices) and then at No. 97 (above). Charlie 'Barmy Bikes' Knight acquired the business in 1958.

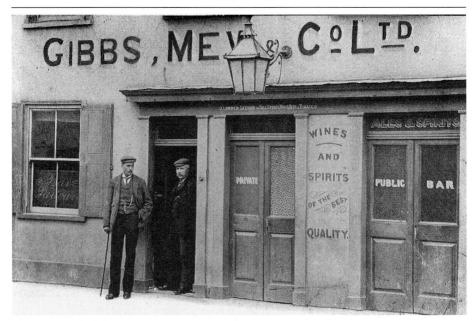

The Kings Arms Inn, before 1906. The Parlour Bar is on the left and the Public Bar is on the right. At this time James Lonnen was the proprietor; in 1897 the landlord was Edgar Pearcey and ten years later the licensee was the very suitably named James Beer.

Waiting for the King, 27 June 1908. The junction of Fisherton Street and South Western Road (formerly Station Road) was festooned with flowers and flags for the royal occasion. Robert Sims of the Plume of Feathers Hotel should have been congratulated for his initiative: 'Royal Visit, Windows to Let; Bed and Breakfast, 3/3'.

The London Inn, 1875. William Harris was the keeper from around 1860 to 1883, and during the following twelve years or so Charles Southcliffe ran the business (then functioning as the London Hotel). In more recent times the establishment was known as the Dorchester Hotel (Sandra Yeates, proprietor), and presently it is Pinocchios Restaurant.

Uphill's Cycle Shop, adjoining the London Hotel. Walter Uphill started out as a cycle agent in around 1915 at Alton House, on the corner of York Road and Sidney Street. By 1927, however, his name could be seen above two shops in Fisherton Street, firstly No. 89 and then No. 137 (above). All three outlets were vacated before 1935.

The smallest shopfront in Salisbury, 1906. Tom Sparks opened this hairdressing salon at 139 Fisherton Street in around 1900. It was a tiny place, with a frontage that was no more than 72 inches wide. By 1908 he had taken on two further branches: 31 Milford Street (formerly Harry Young's) and 9A Winchester Street. An interior view of the Fisherton salon can be seen opposite.

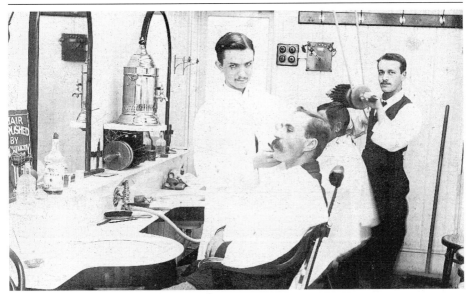

'Hair brushed by machinery'. Securely bolted to the salon ceiling was a powerful motor and a pulley, which in turn was attached to a belt-driven rotary brush (the electrical switch gear can just be seen on the back wall). Gentle downward pressure on the belt set the bristles spinning. One wonders why it did not catch on.

Fisherton Monumental Masonry, before 1906. Stonemason Edward Tabor took over the old established business of Charles James Adey in around 1894. The name Adey is just visible carved into the stonework above the front door. Since 1964 funeral director Derek Shergold has been managing a successful business here.

Fisherton toll-gate, *c.* 1865. Very soon after this remarkable photograph was taken the toll-house was removed, brick by brick, and re-built as Avon Lodge in Old Castle Road (known today as Stratford Road). The building is now used as a veterinary surgery.

This 1920s view of the junction of Fisherton Street with St Paul's Road clearly shows the changes that have occurred. St Paul's roundabout covers much of the foreground today. The toll-gate was situated near the right hand corner.

A final look back. This was the scene at Fisherton Corner on 27 June 1908, when thousands of Wiltshire people converged on Salisbury to catch a glimpse of the King and Queen as they passed through on their way to visit the Pembrokes at Wilton. A multitude of red, white and blue decorations adorned many of the buildings along the route, and all the vantage points were occupied. In the middle of the picture a group of excited children can just be seen peeping over the yard wall at Fisherton School, and, to the right, five women wearing pretty white dresses can be seen taking their places on the roof of no. 1 Wilton Road (Miss King's house). Stretched across the building below them is a banner which briefly, yet precisely, expressed their devotion to the sovereign and his queen: 'Long Live Our King and Queen'.

Acknowledgements

During the past twenty years or so it has been my privilege to meet a very large number of people who have without hesitation shared their experiences of life with me or lent photographs for copying. It would be impossible to name each and every one due to the lack of space here, so my acknowledgements are restricted to those directly involved with this volume. If your contribution does not appear this time then I offer my apologies and hope that you are not too disappointed. Your turn will come. As long as there is a desire for my work I will continue to produce it.

I am especially appreciative of Mr Bill Garrett's significant input throughout the entire compilation of this volume. A gentleman of many experiences, his broad knowledge of old Salisbury is quite unique. My thanks also to Mr Bruce Purvis and Mrs Judith Giles, who so successfully manage our new Salisbury Local Studies Library, a public amenity which I would recommend to those even remotely interested in local or family history. Similarly I am grateful to the following individuals and organizations:

Mrs Sylvia Abel • Fred Amps • Mrs Evelyn Arber • Mrs Joan Arnold
Mrs Rosa Bailey • Les Baker • Nick Baldwin • William Bartlett
Bill Biss • Ron Bracher • Miss Mary Bridle • Mrs Pat Brown • Roger Brown
Mrs Flo Bundy • Maurice Burch • Mrs Barbara Burton • Mrs Joyce Burton
Mrs Joyce Carey • Wilfred E. Chalk • Bill Chick • Patrick Coggan
Tom Dowty • Mrs Dorothy Edwards • Roger Godwin • Miss E.M. Harris
Mrs B. Harrison • Edward Holloway • Peter Hoole • Danny Howell
Frederick James • Mrs Jean Joyce • Charlie Knight • K. de V. and P.E. Lorrain
Mrs Janet Love • E. Arthur Maidment • Mrs Betty McGuinness • S.D. Meaden
Charles Merrifield • Albert Noyce • Colin Oates • Eddie Painter
Mrs Mary Painter • Peter Parrish • Mrs Mary Parsons • Mrs Joan Pepperell
John Pinder • Mrs Edna Pittman • Mrs Jean Pressey • Mike Pugsley
Mrs Phyllis Rose • Reg Rowland • Mrs Marjorie Scott
Derek Shergold • Mrs F. Sherwood • Mrs Mary Smith • Mrs Nellie Smith
David Smith • Graham Stoodley • Arthur Syrett • Henry Topham
Mrs Beryl Wainwright • Dave Ward • Donald Ware • Mrs June Webber
Mrs Eve West • Mrs G. West • Stanley Witcomb • Chas H. Baker & Son
Edwards Brothers • F. Futcher & Son • Hampshire Record Office
Salisbury and South Wiltshire Museum• *Salisbury Journal* • *Salisbury Times*
Southern Evening Echo • *The Avon Advertiser* • Wiltshire Fire Brigade
Wiltshire Record Office.